# MONSTER TRUCKS!
## BIG MACHINES ON THE ROAD

### Vehicles for Kids
### Children's Transportation Books

BABY PROFESSOR

EDUCATION KIDS

Speedy Publishing LLC

40 E. Main St. #1156

Newark, DE 19711

www.speedypublishing.com

Copyright 2018

**I**n this book, we're going to talk about monster trucks. So, let's get right to it!

MONSTER TRUCK

# WHAT IS A MONSTER TRUCK?

At the beginning, regular pickup trucks were changed to create monster trucks. If you've ever seen a monster truck on the road, there's no way of mistaking it. It has a much larger suspension system than a regular pickup truck. It also has enormous tires.

**MONSTER TRUCK DOING A STUNT**

Today, the bodies of pickup trucks are still used to make monster trucks. In monster-truck competitions, other kinds of trucks are used as well. Some have bodies that are like the bodies of sport utility vehicles, known as SUVs.

**S**ome have standard car bodies and some even have bodies designed with animal themes. Generally, the bodies of monster trucks are made of either fiberglass or metal.

MUD BOGGING

# THE HISTORY OF MONSTER TRUCKS

During the 1970s, competitive truck motorsports were becoming very popular. Mud bogging was one of these sports. The goal of mud bogging is to drive a truck through a mud pit. Another popular sport was truck pulling. In this sport, trucks pull very heavy sleds on a track that is 330 feet in length and 35 feet wide. The vehicle that is able to pull the sled over the longest distance wins the competition.

Some of the truck owners who were competing in these sports started to modify their trucks or other vehicles so they would be higher off the ground. Soon, this trend started a competition for who could create the truck that was the biggest.

HOMEBUILT CADILLAC MONSTER TRUCK
GKB313

BIGFOOT

The trucks that gained attention across the United States at that time were:

- Bigfoot, designed by Bob Chandler
- USA-1, designed by Everett Jasmer
- Bear Foot, designed by Fred Shafer and also by Jack Willman, Sr.
- King Kong, designed by Jeff Dane

At that time, the largest tires had 48-inch diameters.

# WHERE DID THE TERM "MONSTER TRUCK" COME FROM?

**B**ob George, who was one of the owners of Truck-a-Rama, a company that promoted truck motorsports, is thought to be the person who came up with the name "monster truck." It was in reference to Bob Chandler's truck Bigfoot and that was when Bigfoot still had 48-inch tires. The term "monster truck" was eventually used for all trucks with special, enormous tires known as terra tires.

JACKED UP 1950'S CAR

AFTERBURNER FLIES HIGH IN MONSTER JAM

Today, Truck-a-Rama is the United States Hot Rod Association (USHRA). The USHRA markets *Monster Jam* and other events for monster trucks and other off-road vehicles.

**M**onster Jam is the largest event for monster trucks in the United States.

# WHO CRUSHED THE FIRST CARS WITH A MONSTER TRUCK?

As a test of the truck's abilities, Bob Chandler drove Bigfoot over some cars in 1981. He had it filmed so he could use it to promote his shop for four-wheel drives. In the video, Bigfoot easily crushed the cars it drove over. By chance, an event manager saw the video and thought the car crush would make a great event. He wanted Bob to perform the drive in front of an audience.

BIGFOOT CRUSHING CARS

2 BIG 4U

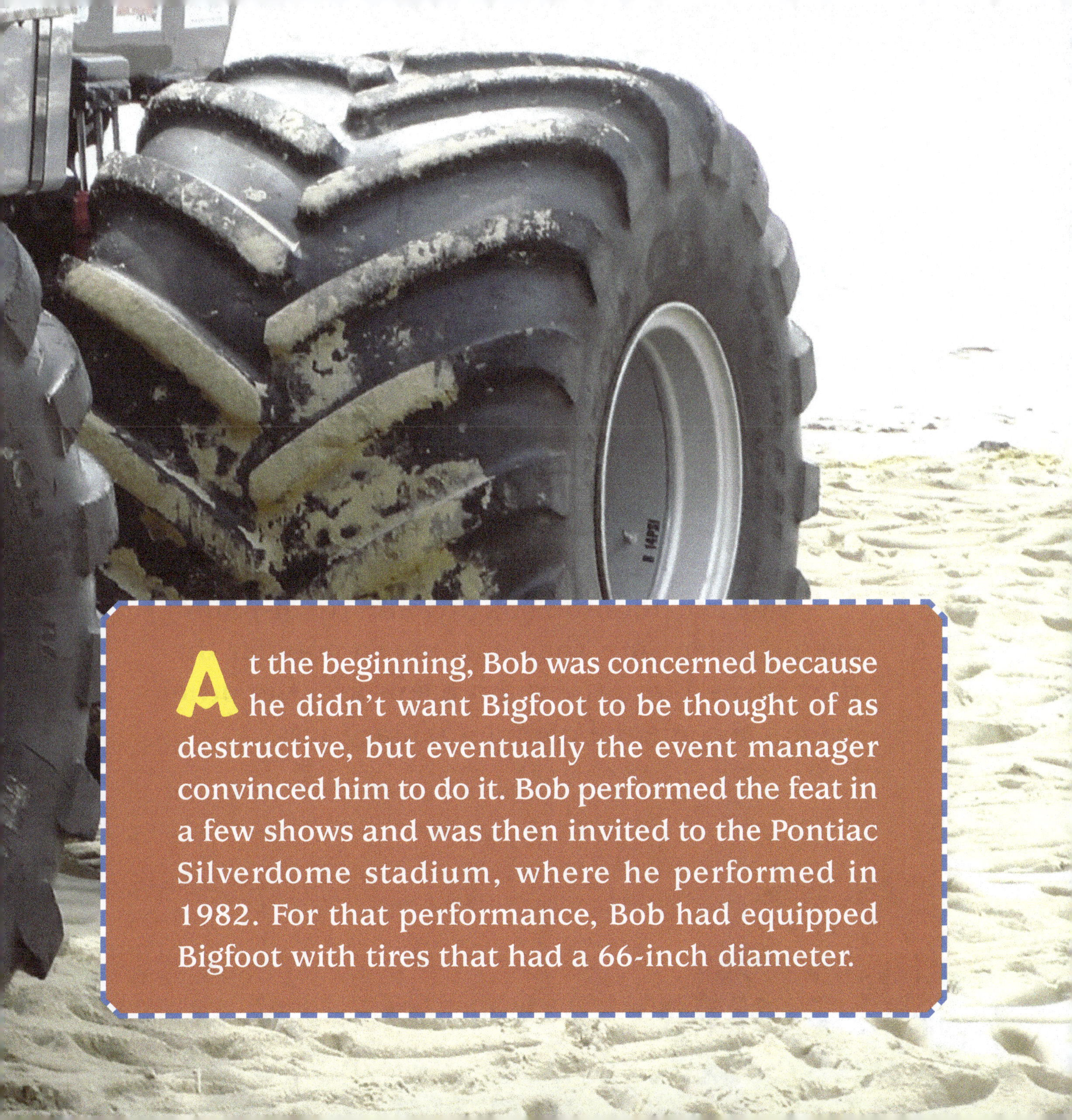

At the beginning, Bob was concerned because he didn't want Bigfoot to be thought of as destructive, but eventually the event manager convinced him to do it. Bob performed the feat in a few shows and was then invited to the Pontiac Silverdome stadium, where he performed in 1982. For that performance, Bob had equipped Bigfoot with tires that had a 66-inch diameter.

# HOW DID MONSTER TRUCKS BECOME THE MAIN EVENT?

At the beginning, monster trucks made up the side acts for mud bogging and truck-pulling events. Over time, they became so popular that they turned into the main event and the other events became the complementary acts.

7 ELEVEN
7 ELEVEN
MUTANT
WHIPLASH MONSTER
TRUCK BACKFLIP

**T**oday, in order to perform in a competition, a monster truck needs to be 12 feet in height and 12 feet in width. Since 2015, monster trucks must also be equipped with tires produced specifically for them by Balkrishna Industries Limited (BKT) in India.

These special 462-lb tires have 66-inch diameters. Because monster trucks are so large, they are very dangerous if they get out of control.

Giant
SPEED BANDIT
MONSTER TRUCK
17

oday, all trucks that compete must have a switch that kills their engines immediately. Track officials have the power to cut the engine if they feel that the truck is unsafe for its driver or for the spectators watching the show.

BIGFOOT 15 CLOSEUP

# WHAT TYPES OF EVENTS DO MONSTER TRUCK SHOWS HAVE?

There are usually two types of major events in a monster truck competition. There's a race followed by a competition that's freestyle.

- The Race Competition
- The Freestyle Competition

## The Race Competition

The races are a type of tournament that's described as "single elimination." In each round of the race, two trucks are paired in a competition on separate tracks.

These dirt tracks are symmetrical and whichever truck wins then moves on to the next round of the event. Usually, the short tracks have a steep turn and an enormous jump over cars organized in a row.

## The Freestyle Competition

Since 2017, the freestyle segment of the event is always last. For several years, the events included school buses or motor homes being crushed. However, there were injuries and deaths from flying debris so this practice was changed.

MONSTER TRUCK DURING A FREESTYLE COMPETITION

U.S. AIR FORCE
AFTERBURNER
Cross Into The Blue
U.S. AIR FORCE
AIRFORCE.COM
1-800-423-USAF
U.S. AIR FORCE
AIR FORCE
AIR FORCE

The tracks for freestyle have huge jumps and specially designed ramps so that the monster trucks can make powerful wheelies when they land. For safety reasons, only one truck is performing on the track during a freestyle event. These performances are timed and the judges give points for each stunt. The driver who accumulates the most points awarded by the judges wins the event.

CHAMPION
1
MONSTER
TRUCK
GO! GO!

# WHAT WINS POINTS DURING FREESTYLE?

**J**udges use a scoring system as they determine the points for each driver. Here are some of the actions that a skilled driver performs during freestyle that can win points with the judges.

- Performing lots of different tricks
- Crashing into the most obstacles placed on the tracks
- Doing donuts, which means spinning in circles in one location

- Doing a cyclone donut, which means a very high-speed donut
- Performing a "wow-factor" stunt that everyone would think is impossible

- Driving skillfully to stop a crash or roll over from happening
- Driving on two of the side wheels until the truck gets back in balance

- Doing wheelies, which means driving on the back wheels only with the front wheels in the air
- Doing sky wheelies, which means the rear tires are on the ground and the front wheels are straight up in the air with the truck at a 90-degree angle to the ground
- Doing multiple tricks in just one pass

FOWLER
FAMILY
FAIR
EST. 1886
The CHAMP
CHAMPION
Michael's
UNWANTED

GraveDigger
GRAVE DIGGER

# WHAT GETS DEDUCTIONS DURING FREESTYLE?

- Stopping
- Rolling over
- Backing up

# THE PARTS OF A MONSTER TRUCK

At 12-feet tall and 12-feet wide, a monster truck designed for competition weighs around 10 thousand pounds! Advanced engineering technology has made it possible for these big machines to have specially built bodies and custom-made tires so their drivers can be safe without sacrificing the truck's maneuverability or speed.

## Truck Body

Most monster trucks today have custom-made bodies. Styrofoam, wood, and plaster are used to create a mold for the custom design, which is generally made from fiberglass.

The designers who make the body use advanced techniques of computer software in combination with carving by hand. Each truck has a special character or a specific theme.

## Driver's Seat

The driver's seat is located in the center of the truck so the driver can easily see the track. This position is also best for the truck's interior weight distribution. To keep the driver as safe as possible, the seats are molded to fit the driver's body securely.

There are devices to keep the heads and necks of the drivers restrained so they won't get hurt when the truck slams down from a great height. There are also special seatbelts with 5-point harnesses to keep the driver's body still.

# Engine

Monster truck engines use methanol fuel. Up to 2.5 gallons are burned up on every run of 250 feet of track. The engines have 1,500 horsepower.

Las Vegas
CONVENT
MOTHERS
California Gold
Carnauba
Cleaner Wax
MOTHERS
California Gold
ClayBar
MOTHERS
California Gold
ClayBar
MOTHERS
California Gold
Showtime
SIN CITY
CRUSHER
GATORWRAPS.CO
SKIN FOR YOUR
WWW.MONSTER-STYLE.COM
HERS
HERS
Cleaner

## Artwork Design

It can require up to 40 hours to produce the detailed artwork that embellishes the outside of the monster truck's body. Sometimes detailed decals are used as well. Painters as well as decal installers are always busy because during the shows the paint jobs are almost always destroyed.

# Suspension System

The suspension system is critical in a monster truck. Each tire has two dedicated 30-inch-long shock absorbers. They are filled with both oil as well as nitrogen gas to soften the impact of jumping the ramps and crashing into obstacles.

# Tires

A monster truck will burn through 8 tires annually. The tires are 66 inches in diameter and the width of the tires is 43 inches.

# MONSTER TRUCKS HELP IN MONSTER-SIZED FLOODS

Because monster trucks are so high off the ground's surface, over the last few years they have been used to help rescue people in areas with massive floods.

OSHKOSH
USMC 596259
SUPPLY
M14301
TIE DOWN

# SUMMARY

Monster trucks started as regular pickup trucks that were transformed with larger suspension systems and larger tires. When Bob Chandler drove his first monster truck called "Bigfoot" across two parked cars and crushed them, a new sport was born. Today, monster truck events across the world thrill spectators as they perform stunts with their huge 66-inch tires. In addition to being used for entertainment, monster trucks have sometimes been used to help people get out of flooded areas.

CASCADEUR MONSTER TRUCK

wesome! Now that you've read about monster trucks, you may want to read more about other big machines in the Baby Professor book, *Trucks, Trains and Big Machines!*

Visit
BABY PROFESSOR
EDUCATION KIDS
www.BabyProfessorBooks.com
to download Free Baby Professor eBooks and view
our catalog of new and exciting Children's Books